ESTD 2017

KIDS LIGHTHOUSE

ALL FOR HIS GLORY

To:_____
_____

From:_____
_____

The Great Commission

HI THERE. MY NAME IS SQUASH. IF YOU HAVEN'T GUESSED BY NOW, I'M A BABY OCTOPUS.

I WAS PUT IN THIS BEAUTIFUL OCEAN BY THE SAME GOD WHO MADE YOU!

HE MUST REALLY LOVE US!

I AM ABOUT TO TELL YOU A WONDERFUL, BEAUTIFUL, SPECTACULAR, AND AMAZING STORY!

ARE YOU READY?

IT ALL STARTED WHEN I WAS SWIMMING THROUGH THE OCEAN. I LOVE SWIMMING. DO YOU LOVE SWIMMING? I KNOW, I TALK A LOT, BUT I CAN'T HELP IT, I JUST HAVE SO MUCH TO SAY!

SO AS I WAS SWIMMING, I WAS SINGING A SONG. I LOVE SINGING, DO YOU LOVE SINGING? I LOVE A LOT OF THINGS. LIFE IS JUST SO BEAUTIFUL!

SO AS I WAS SINGING A SONG...

OH, I FORGOT TO TELL YOU THE SONG THAT I WAS SINGING! THE SONG I WAS SINGING WAS JESUS LOVES ME. DO YOU KNOW IT? I LOVE JESUS. DO YOU LOVE JESUS?

SO AS I WAS SWIMMING AND
SINGING JESUS LOVES ME, I CAME
ACROSS THE CUTEST, THE MOST
ADORABLE, THE MOST TINY, AND
THE MOST ITSY BITSY SEAHORSE! I
LOVE SEAHORSES, DO YOU LOVE
SEAHORSES?

WHEN I SAW HIM, THIS IS WHAT I SAID.

HELLO BABY SEAHORSE. I'M A BABY OCTOPUS AND I HAVE 8 ARMS. I LOVE SWIMMING, SINGING, JESUS, LIFE, PIZZA, GUMMY WORMS, THE SKY, THE CLOUDS...

BUT THEN HE STOPPED ME BEFORE
I COULD FINISH. HE SAID THESE
WORDS TO ME.

YOU SURE DO TALK A LOT.

SO I SAID...
WHO ME?

I THEN LAUGHED, BECAUSE I LOVE
TALKING. SOMETIMES I COULD JUST
TALK AND TALK AND TALK AND TALK.
DO YOU LOVE TALKING?

HE THEN ASKED ME THIS.
I LOVE ALL OF THOSE THINGS TOO,
BUT WHO IS JESUS?

I LET OUT A GREAT BIG GASP AND SAID THIS.
YOU DON'T KNOW WHO JESUS IS?
I THOUGHT EVERYONE KNOWS WHO JESUS IS!

I THEN TOLD HIM ALL OF THE MANY BEAUTIFUL THINGS ABOUT JESUS, AND HOW MUCH HE LOVES US ALL. I TOLD HIM A LOT, BECAUSE IF YOU HAVEN'T NOTICED BY NOW, I TALK A LOT, AND WHEN I TALK A LOT, I KEEP GOING AND GOING AND GOING AND GOING AND...

SORRY, I'M DOING IT AGAIN, AREN'T I?

AFTER I FINISHED TALKING TO THE BABY SEAHORSE, HE WAS SO IN LOVE WITH JESUS TOO! THE BIBLE TELLS US TO TELL OTHERS ABOUT WHO JESUS IS. SOME PEOPLE HAVE NEVER EVEN HEARD OF JESUS! IT'S OUR JOB TO SHARE HOW AMAZING JESUS IS! THIS IS CALLED THE GREAT COMMISSION.

AFTER I TOLD THE BABY SEAHORSE ABOUT JESUS, I WAS SO HAPPY! I WANTED TO TELL MORE CREATURES ABOUT JESUS. I WAS NOW ON A MISSION FOR THE GREAT COMMISSION! I LOVE RHYMING. DO YOU LOVE RHYMING?

I THEN SET OUT ON MY MISSION TO TELL MORE CREATURES ABOUT MY BEAUTIFUL AND WONDERFUL JESUS!

AS I WAS SWIMMING AND TALKING AND SWIMMING AND TALKING AND TALKING AND SWIMMING, I MET THE CUTEST, MOST PLAYFUL BABY TURTLE! HE WAS SO ADORABLE!

I TOLD HIM ALL ABOUT MY JESUS.

HE THEN ASKED ME HOW MY JESUS
CAN BE HIS JESUS TOO.

AFTER I SHARED A SCRIPTURE IN ROMANS 10:9-10, HE BELIEVED IN JESUS TOO! SO MY JESUS, BECAME HIS JESUS TOO! WE ARE NOW BOTH CHILDREN OF GOD.

THE NEXT THING HE SAID SHOCKED ME!

HE SAID HE WAS GOING TO FOLLOW
THE GREAT COMMISSION TOO!

THIS MADE ME SO HAPPY!

SO WE SAID OUR GOODBYES, AND OFF HE WENT TO SHARE THE GOOD NEWS OF JESUS!

I HAD A SUPER LONG DAY TODAY. I TALKED A LOT MORE THAN I USUALLY TALK, AND I USUALLY TALK A LOT. I TALK A LOT MORE THAN MOST CREATURES TALK, BECAUSE I LIKE TO TALK A LOT.

AS I WAS ON MY WAY HOME, I SAW A FRIEND FROM MY SCHOOL. WE CALL HIM COOL BLUE, BECAUSE HE LOOKS DIFFERENT THAN MOST OCTOPUS. I LOVE BEING DIFFERENT, DO YOU LOVE BEING DIFFERENT?

I NEVER TOLD HIM ABOUT JESUS BEFORE, AND I DECIDED TO KEEP FOLLOWING THE GREAT COMMISSION, SO I TOLD HIM ALL ABOUT JESUS.

HE WAS SO IN SHOCK THAT HIS EYES LOOKED LIKE THEY WERE HUGE! HE COULDN'T BELIEVE THAT JESUS LOVED HIM SO MUCH. I TOLD HIM THAT IT'S BECAUSE JESUS LOVES US WITH A BEAUTIFUL PERFECT LOVE!

HE WAS SO HAPPY THAT HIS EYES
SQUIRT WATER UNDER WATER!
THEY WERE HAPPY TEARS.

HE ASKED ME TO PRAY WITH HIM, SO I DID. AND SO, ANOTHER CREATURE WAS ADDED TO THE MISSION OF THE GREAT COMMISSION.

THE END.

WAIT! I FORGOT TO TELL YOU SOMETHING.

I LEARNED THAT HE LOVES PIZZA TOO! I LOVE PIZZA, DO YOU LOVE PIZZA?

And He said to them, "Go into all the world and preach the gospel to every creature.

Mark 16:15

Therefore go and make disciples of all nations, baptizing them in the name of the Father and of the Son and of the Holy Spirit, and teaching them to obey everything I have commanded you. And surely I am with you always, to the very end of the age."

Matthew 28:19-20

JESUS WANTS US TO TELL OTHERS ABOUT HIM. IF NO ONE SHARES THE LOVE OF JESUS, HOW CAN ANYONE EVER KNOW WHO HE IS? WILL YOU BE MY FRIEND AND JOIN ME IN FOLLOWING THE MISSION OF THE GREAT COMMISSION?

The Great Commission